THE ADVENTURES OF MERLIN

ARTHUR
AND THE UNICORN

LEVEL 1

SCHOLASTIC

Adapted by: Lynda Edwards
Based on the screenplay by Howard Overman
Series created by Julian Jones, Jake Michie, Julian Murphy and Johnny Capps.

Publisher: Jacquie Bloese

Editor: Fiona Davis

Designer: Dawn Wilson

Cover layout: Dawn Wilson

Picture research: Pupak Navabpour

Photo credits:
Cover and interior images © 2009 Shine Limited.
Pages 34 & 35: F Mayer, A Woolfitt, Bettmann/Corbis; Mary Evans Picture Library.
Pages 36 & 37: Mary Evans Picture Library; Paramount, Disney/Allstar; INTERFOTO/Alamy.

Published by Scholastic Ltd. 2010

Mary Glasgow Magazines (Scholastic Ltd.)
Euston House
24 Eversholt Street
London NW1 IDB

Printed in Malaysia

Reprinted in 2010, 2011, 2013, 2014 and 2015

CONTENTS PAGE

MERLIN

Merlin is Arthur's young servant and friend. He lives with Gaius. Merlin is also a wizard, but only Gaius knows this. Merlin is clever and funny and wants to help Arthur.

ARTHUR PENDRAGON

Arthur is the King's son. One day he is going to be King of Camelot. He's young and good-looking. He loves his father and his people. Sometimes he doesn't think before he does things.

UTHER PENDRAGON

Uther is the King of Camelot. He's a proud man and wants Camelot to be strong. He hates magic.

GAIUS

Gaius is the King's doctor and old friend. He teaches Merlin many things about life. He's a kind man.

ANHORA

Anhora is a very special kind of wizard. He protects the unicorns.

The UNICORN is a magical animal.

PLACES

CAMELOT is the kingdom > of Uther Pendragon and Arthur. It is a very beautiful place.

THE LABYRINTH OF GEDREF is a strange, magical place. It is difficult to find a way through.

ARTHUR AND THE UNICORN

PROLOGUE

Young Merlin left his home in the country. He went to live with Gaius in the city of Camelot. Gaius was an old friend of his mother's. Merlin had a lot to learn about life in the city – and Gaius helped him. Merlin was good at magic but only Gaius knew this. The King did not like to have magic in Camelot.

When Merlin first met Arthur, he did not like him. But the Great Dragon spoke to Merlin. 'One day Arthur is going to be a great king. But he cannot do this without you, Merlin. You must protect and help him.'

CHAPTER 1
THE UNICORN

It was quiet in the forest. The men watched and waited. White light danced through the trees and on their faces. They were ready to kill.

Arthur spoke quietly to Merlin. 'Look,' he said. 'Something white. In the trees. Go in there. When the animal runs, I can kill it.'

Merlin left the others and walked into the trees. He wasn't happy. He didn't like killing. It was dark too, and he was frightened. Perhaps it was a big animal. But Arthur was the King's son. When Arthur said something, Merlin did it.

Suddenly he stopped. Was this a dream? There was a white light in front of him. In the centre of the light there was a beautiful animal, tall and strong. It was white and a long horn came from its head. It was a unicorn, the most magical animal in the world.

Merlin heard a sound behind him. He turned. It was Arthur. And his eyes were on the unicorn.

'No, Arthur!' shouted Merlin. But it was too late. There

was a terrible cry and the unicorn was on the forest floor.

Merlin put his hand on the unicorn's head. 'I'm so sorry,' he said.

The unicorn looked at him with sad eyes. Merlin watched as the unicorn moved for the last time.

Arthur laughed. 'Fantastic – a unicorn! You don't see them very often!'

'Why did you do this? It isn't right,' said Merlin sadly.

'Don't be a girl, Merlin!' Arthur took the long horn from the dead unicorn's head. Behind him, Merlin saw someone in the trees. It was an old man in white clothes. His face was both angry and sad.

'What are you looking at?' Arthur said. He turned, but there was no one there.

★ ★ ★

Arthur and Merlin took the unicorn's horn to Uther Pendragon. The King was pleased with his son. He looked at the unicorn's horn and smiled.

'This is good, Arthur!' he said. He gave it to his old friend and doctor, Gaius. 'What do you think, Gaius?'

Gaius wasn't happy. 'My Lord*, unicorns are magical animals. There is an old story. Bad things can happen when a unicorn dies.'

But Uther didn't believe him. 'You're wrong, Gaius! This horn is going to be lucky for Camelot!' He and Arthur left the room.

Merlin turned to Gaius. 'The unicorn was so beautiful,' he told the old man.

Gaius smiled at him. 'You were lucky, Merlin. Not many people see a unicorn.'

'But it died in front of me,' Merlin said sadly.

★ ★ ★

Merlin looked out of the window of Arthur's room. He was very quiet.

Arthur looked over at him. 'What's the problem, Merlin? Are you still thinking about that unicorn?'

'It was wrong, Arthur. I know it!'

* People used *My Lord* when they spoke to the King or his son.

'Oh – and you know everything!' Arthur laughed. 'We were in the forest to kill animals – not to find pets!'

Merlin didn't say anything. The picture of the dead unicorn was still in his head.

Arthur went over to him. 'Look, Merlin, you are my servant. Your job is to clean my room. Don't talk to me about right and wrong! Now, come on! This room is dirty – and there's a rat. Find it and kill it!'

Just then the door opened. 'My Lord,' said the man. 'There is a problem. The King needs you. Now.'

* * *

Uther was in a cornfield by the city walls. All around him the corn was dry and yellow.

'It's dead, Arthur. It's all dead.'

Arthur looked around him. 'But I don't understand, Father. Yesterday I was here. Everything was green. The corn was fine then.'

Uther looked at his son. His face was white. 'We have a very big problem, Arthur. It's not only happening here.'

'What do you mean, Father?'

'It's the same all over the kingdom. Everywhere the corn is dead or dying. The people cannot make bread. The animals have nothing to eat. The people of Camelot are going to die.'

CHAPTER 2
ANHORA

'I tested the corn, Merlin, but I don't understand. Why did it die so quickly?' Gaius was a clever doctor but he didn't have an answer for this problem.

Merlin looked at him. His eyes were dark. 'I think it's magic.'

★ ★ ★

In the storeroom, Uther and Arthur looked at the bags of corn. There weren't very many.

'Each family has a little every day,' said Uther coldly. 'No one takes more, or they die.'

Suddenly Gaius and Merlin ran in. They were frightened.

'My Lord! Now there is no water!' Gaius told the King.

'What?' Uther was angry. 'My people are hungry. They can't live without water. Why is this happening, Gaius?'

'There's only one answer,' Gaius said slowly. 'It's magic.'

Uther closed his eyes. 'I knew it,' he said. 'Someone wants Camelot to fall.'

★ ★ ★

Merlin read from his magic book. '*Greot gecumean leccan,**' he said quietly.

Gaius came in the room and smiled. 'We need your magic, Merlin. Can you do it? Can you stop the curse?'

'No, Gaius. This magic is stronger than mine.'

★ ★ ★

It was dark. Arthur went back to the storeroom. Merlin followed him. Suddenly Arthur stopped. There was someone there.

'Come on, Merlin,' said Arthur quietly. The two young men ran into the storeroom. It was dark and cold. It was also very quiet. Someone's watching us, thought Merlin. He didn't like the feeling. They walked slowly through the rooms. They were empty.

Suddenly something moved in the dark.

'Quick, Merlin!' shouted Arthur. 'You go that way! Then he can't get out!'

Arthur ran one way and Merlin ran the other. Merlin was frightened. Who was it? What did he want? But then Arthur was in front of him again.

'Did you see him? Where is he?' Arthur was excited.

'No, I didn't see anyone!'

'What? That's not possible. He went this way!' Arthur walked round the rooms again. He didn't understand it.

'Are you looking for me?'

Arthur turned. Merlin's heart almost stopped. There was an old man behind them. He was in white clothes and

* Merlin is speaking a magical language.

he didn't smile. It was the man from the forest.

'I am Anhora. I protect the unicorns. My words are for you, Arthur Pendragon.'

Arthur's eyes were cold. Did this man use magic? 'Was it you?' he asked angrily. 'Did you kill the corn and take away the water?'

'No, Arthur,' said Anhora quietly. 'It was you.'

Now there was fire in Arthur's eyes. 'Me? Do you think that I want to kill my own people?' He put his hand on his sword.

Anhora didn't move. 'The curse came to Camelot because you killed the unicorn.'

Arthur pulled out his sword. '*You* put the curse on Camelot. Take it away or die!'

'That is not possible,' said the old man.

Arthur moved towards him but then the man wasn't there. Where did he go?

'I have some tests for you, Arthur.' Arthur and Merlin turned. Anhora was at the door. 'You must pass the tests or Camelot falls.'

Then the storeroom was empty. Arthur and Merlin were alone in the dark again.

CHAPTER 3
THE FIRST TEST

'I'm sorry, Merlin. There's not much for breakfast.' Gaius put some food and a cup of tea in front of the young man.

Merlin was surprised. 'Tea! Where did you find the water?' He started to drink it.

Gaius gave him a small smile. 'It's your bath water – from yesterday. It was still in the bath!'

Merlin put his hand over his mouth. Suddenly he wasn't thirsty!

Gaius looked carefully at Merlin. 'We only have this water now. You must talk to Arthur about the curse. He must do something.'

★ ★ ★

'Look, Merlin! The rat is eating my things!' Arthur showed Merlin his shoe. He wasn't happy. 'I can't wear this!'

Merlin smiled. 'Maybe it's hungry – like us!'

Arthur looked at his servant. Was he laughing at him? 'Do you think this is funny?' Arthur walked round the room. He was angry. Merlin watched him. He knew Arthur was really angry about the curse. Arthur wanted to do something. He wanted to help his people.

'What are you going to do about Anhora?' Merlin asked.

Arthur stopped. 'I'm going to find him. Then he's going to take away this curse.'

'But maybe his words were true, Arthur,' Merlin said quietly.

Arthur's face was red. 'Do you think all this is because of me?'

'Arthur, listen,' said Merlin. 'Anhora was in the forest

when you killed the unicorn. I didn't tell you because it was like a dream.'

'So?' said Arthur.

'So maybe it's true!'

Arthur closed his ears to Merlin's words. He didn't want to believe him. The thought was terrible. He loved Camelot and its people. He thought about the unicorn and the horn. He remembered the lovely, white body and the dark, dead eyes.

'No!' shouted Arthur angrily. 'Anhora is a wizard. I don't believe him. He wants to kill my people. It was Anhora, not me!'

Merlin looked at Arthur. His eyes were sad. 'I believe him,' he said.

'Then you are stupid!' Arthur looked away quickly. 'You must never believe a wizard. My father told me that.' He took his coat. 'Now, come with me. I'm going to find Anhora and take him to my father. This time he isn't going to run away.'

★ ★ ★

In the dark storeroom, Arthur and Merlin waited for Anhora. Merlin sat on the floor. He was tired. He closed his eyes.

Arthur wasn't pleased. 'I'm happy that you can sleep, Merlin! Everyone is hungry and thirsty – but you – you just go to sleep.' Suddenly Arthur was quiet. He saw a light under the door. 'Someone's coming!' he said. 'I knew it! Anhora is here again.'

The light moved through the different rooms. Quietly Arthur and Merlin followed. In the last room they stopped. Arthur moved forward. He pulled out his sword.

'Come out!' he shouted. They waited. Then there was a sound. A man's white face looked at them from the dark. He had a small bag of corn in his hand.

'Who are you?' asked Arthur.

The man was small and frightened. His face was dirty and his clothes were poor. He looked at the floor.

'I'm Evan, my Lord. I have three children. They're hungry.'

'Everyone is hungry!' Arthur's words were cold. 'It's wrong to take the corn.'

'I know. I'm sorry. I don't want my children to die.'

'And do you want them to lose their father?'

Evan started crying. Arthur was sad. This wasn't easy. Yes, it was wrong to take the corn but this man had a family. His children needed him.

'Go then,' said Arthur quietly. 'Go home!'

Evan looked up. 'Thank you, my Lord,' he said. He put down the corn and started to leave the room.

'Wait!' said Arthur. He gave him the small bag. 'Take this, but don't come back!'

Evan smiled at Arthur. 'You are a good man, my Lord,' he said. 'Camelot thanks you.'

CHAPTER 4
ARTHUR'S PRIDE

The next morning, the people of Camelot were very happy. There was water again. How did it happen? No one knew.

Merlin and Arthur had their first drinks of water. Arthur closed his eyes to enjoy the cold water in his mouth.

'My mouth was so dry,' said Merlin. 'It was difficult to speak!'

Arthur laughed. 'That's one good thing then! But I still don't understand it.'

Merlin was quiet.

'Don't tell me!' said Arthur. 'Merlin knows. Why do you think we have water now? Come on, let's hear it!'

Merlin gave a big smile. 'Anhora talked about tests. Last night in the storeroom, you didn't kill that man. Maybe that was a test. You passed the test and now we have water! Remember his words: "Camelot thanks you!"'

Arthur looked at his servant. Was Merlin right?

'And I know you never listen to me but ...'

Arthur laughed. 'That's true!'

'Arthur, you really can help the people of Camelot.'

'Find some food for me!' Arthur said quickly. 'I'm hungry.' He left the room.

Find food, thought Merlin. Oh yes, Arthur – that's easy! Where can I find some food? Suddenly something moved in Arthur's shoe on the floor. It was the rat! Merlin smiled. Oh yes! Now he had some food!

★ ★ ★

Arthur looked at the dinner in front of him.

'How can I eat when my people have no food?' He looked up. 'Tomorrow we're going to the forest, Merlin,' he said. 'Maybe Anhora is there.'

'Then you must eat,' said Merlin. 'You must be strong.'

Arthur started to eat. 'This meat is different, Merlin. What is it?'

Merlin didn't say anything. He cleaned the table.

Suddenly Arthur stopped eating and looked at Merlin. 'Is it rat?' he asked.

'Mmm,' said Merlin quickly and started to clean the floor.

'But, Merlin!' Arthur was on his feet. 'I'm sure you're hungry, too. You must have some of this lovely meat!' Arthur gave Merlin his food. 'Eat it!'

Merlin thought of the little animal in Arthur's shoe. He closed his eyes and put the food in his mouth. It was terrible!

'Lovely!' he said.

★ ★ ★

The forest was quiet. Is Anhora watching us? thought Merlin. Arthur looked carefully at the forest floor. 'Someone was here,' he told Merlin. Suddenly Arthur saw Anhora in the trees. 'Merlin! Merlin! He's here!' he shouted and started to follow the old man. But Anhora moved very quickly and Arthur was soon alone in the heart of the forest.

Then he saw a small fire. A man sat next to it. It was Evan. There were big bags of food around him. Evan smiled. It was not a nice smile.

'You?' Arthur was surprised. 'Did you take all this food?'

Evan laughed loudly. 'You believed my story! Your people have no food but you still didn't stop me! You're not going to be a good king.'

Arthur was angry but he wanted to find Anhora. 'I must go,' he said.

'Tell me …' said Evan. He came close to Arthur. His eyes were small and cold. 'What does the King think of his stupid son?'

Arthur wanted to go but he had fire in his heart. He was Arthur, son of Uther Pendragon.

'Maybe you're *not* Uther's son!' Evan laughed again, long and loud.

Quickly, Arthur pulled out his sword. This man must die! Evan pulled out his sword, too. Arthur hit Evan's sword but the man was strong. He came back again and again. Then suddenly Evan's sword was on the floor. Arthur moved to kill him. His sword went through nothing! Impossible! Evan wasn't there. Arthur turned. Where was he? He turned again. No one!

Then he saw Anhora. The old man's eyes were cold. Oh no, thought Arthur. Now I understand. 'Was this your test?' he asked quietly.

'Yes, Arthur. Why did you kill this man?'

Arthur was angry again. 'Because he laughed at me!'

'Is your pride more important than a man's life?'

Arthur looked down sadly. Another mistake. What was wrong with him? Why didn't he learn? 'Please Anhora, please! Take the curse away,' cried Arthur. 'My people did nothing wrong. It was me.'

'It is too late, Arthur. Camelot must pay for this.'

CHAPTER 5
THE LAST TEST

When Arthur and Merlin returned to Camelot, the King met them. His face was dark. 'The last corn in the storeroom is bad. We can't eat it. There is no more food for the people.'

'Then we must go to other kingdoms and ask the kings for food,' said his son.

'No, Arthur,' said Uther. 'The other kingdoms must not know.'

'Why?' Arthur was angry. 'Can't you see? Our people are dying. We need help.'

'Never!' shouted Uther. 'You are my son, Arthur! Where is your pride?'

Arthur heard the word 'pride' and he remembered Anhora's words: 'Is your pride more important than a man's life?'

'I cannot think of my pride, Father. Not when our people are hungry.' Arthur turned away and walked out of the room.

'There is no more food,' Uther shouted after him.

'Then *you* must tell the people,' said Arthur.

★ ★ ★

A lot of people waited in the streets of Camelot. They were all hungry and they hoped for food. Arthur and Merlin watched them.

'What can I do, Merlin?' said Arthur sadly. 'There is no food. It's the end for all these people. And it is all because of my pride.'

Arthur cared about his people. Merlin knew that. 'It was a difficult test, Arthur,' he said.

'I was stupid, Merlin, stupid! Evan was right. I'm not going to be a good king.'

★ ★ ★

Merlin went back to the forest. This time he was alone. He wanted to talk to Anhora about Arthur. He wanted to tell him about his friend's love for his people.

Suddenly Merlin saw the magical white light again. 'Anhora! Where are you?' he shouted. His words came back to him from the trees. Then it was quiet again. The forest was empty. Sadly Merlin turned to leave.

'What do you want to say to me?' The old man was in front of him.

Merlin tried to find the right words. 'Help us please, Anhora. The people are dying. Arthur was wrong but he's sorry. He has a good heart. Give Arthur another test.'

Anhora saw the light and hope in Merlin's eyes. He loved his friend. 'Do you really believe in Arthur?' Anhora asked.

'Yes,' said Merlin. 'I do.'

'Then Arthur must go to the Labyrinth of Gedref. He must pass the last test. Then the curse can end. Tell Arthur this,' said Anhora.

And then Merlin was alone again in the dark forest.

CHAPTER 6
THE LABYRINTH OF GEDREF

'I want to come with you. You need me, Arthur!' Merlin didn't want Arthur to go to Gedref alone.

'No, Merlin. I have one last test. I thank you for that. But it is *my* test. Stay here. Help the people.'

Arthur left Camelot. What waited for him at Gedref? He didn't know. Merlin decided to follow Arthur to Gedref. He wanted to protect him.

★ ★ ★

The Labyrinth of Gedref was very big. Arthur looked in. It was very dark. He must find the way through. Arthur went in with his sword in his hand. The lines of trees closed around him. He walked quickly. He wanted to pass this test and help his people.

Merlin followed Arthur into the Labyrinth. But he went a different way. He ran one way. Then he ran another. Each way looked the same. And he was alone. Where was Arthur?

Suddenly Merlin was in the centre of the Labyrinth. But he wasn't alone now. There was something white against the dark green trees. It was Anhora. His eyes were black and he had a sword in his hands.

'What are you doing? Are you waiting for Arthur?' shouted Merlin.

'No, Merlin,' said Anhora. 'I am waiting for you. *Gehaeftan*!' Suddenly green arms came out of the trees and went round Merlin. Everything went dark.

★ ★ ★

Arthur was at the end of the Labyrinth. The trees opened and there was light again. He moved forward and looked round.

It was like a dream. He was on a small beach. There was a table with two chairs. One chair was empty. On the other chair sat Merlin! Anhora was behind him.

'Merlin must go, Anhora!' shouted Arthur. 'It's my test, not his!'

'That is not possible. Merlin is part of your test. Please, sit!'

Arthur sat down slowly. 'All right!' He looked at Anhora. His head was high. 'What's the test?' I can do this, he thought. I must do this.

'There are two cups on the table,' said Anhora. 'There is water in both. But in one there is also poison. You must drink all the water from both cups. But each of you can drink from one cup only.'

Arthur was angry. 'That's a stupid test! What can it tell you?'

'You must decide that, Arthur.'

Merlin looked at Arthur and then at the cups. 'Let's think carefully, Arthur. I drink from this cup ...'

'... and you die.'

'Or you drink from yours and you die!'

'It's very easy,' said Arthur. 'One of us is going to die. We find the cup with the poison in it and then I drink it.'

'No, I drink it!'

'No. It was my mistake. I killed the unicorn. I die!'

Merlin looked at Arthur. 'You mustn't die, Arthur. You're going to be a great king.'

'Do you really want to die for me?' asked Arthur. He tried to laugh. 'I had no idea!'

'It's a surprise to me, too!' said Merlin.

There was love for his friend in Arthur's eyes. 'I'm happy you're here, Merlin,' he said.

Suddenly Merlin had an idea. 'I know! We put the water from one cup into the other. Then we know *that* cup has the poison in it!'

'Not bad, Merlin,' Arthur smiled.

Suddenly he was on his feet. 'Be careful!' he shouted.

Merlin looked behind him and Arthur quickly put all the water in one cup. Merlin turned back. The cup was at Arthur's mouth.

'No, Arthur!' he shouted. 'Listen to me!'

'I never listen to you, Merlin. You know that!' Arthur finished the water and put the empty cup on the table. He looked at his friend for the last time and smiled sadly. Then his eyes closed.

'No!' cried Merlin. 'Anhora, take me! He mustn't die!' But Arthur didn't move.

CHAPTER 7
The End Of The Curse

'Why did you do this?' Merlin cried. He had his arms round Arthur.

'He's not dead,' said Anhora.

Merlin looked up. He didn't understand.

Anhora's eyes were kind. 'It wasn't a poison. He's only sleeping. He's going to be with us again soon.'

'But why?'

'A unicorn has only love in its heart. The killer of a unicorn must find love in his heart, too. Arthur wanted to give his life for you, Merlin. He has love in his heart. It's the end of the curse.'

* * *

Arthur and Merlin were back at the forest. It was dark and quiet. Nothing moved. Arthur put the unicorn's horn on the forest floor. It was white against the dark brown and green. 'I'm sorry,' he said quietly. 'It was wrong to end your life.'

Then Merlin heard a sound. He turned. 'Arthur! Look!'

Arthur looked up. There was a white light through the trees. In the centre of the light was the unicorn. It looked at them for a long time. Then it slowly moved away into the forest.

Merlin and Arthur heard Anhora. His words came from the trees. 'Arthur, you found love in your heart. Now the unicorn can live again.'

Arthur turned to his friend and smiled. And in Camelot the cornfields were green again.

Merlin The TV Show

***Merlin* arrived on TV in the UK in 2008. Now people all around the world watch it and it's a big hit. It's fun, funny and the story has lots of surprises!**

A new story

The film makers wanted to make a new, exciting TV show about the famous King Arthur stories. In the stories, Merlin is an old wizard and Arthur is a strong king. In *Merlin*, we see Arthur and Merlin when they are both young men. Two new young actors, Colin Morgan (23) and Bradley James (25), play Merlin and Arthur.

The actors

Bradley James plays Arthur. Bradley loves sport. 'I'd love to be a footballer but I'm an actor at the moment,' he jokes. 'I loved working on Merlin. I enjoyed the sword work the best.

Colin (Merlin) was very quiet at first and I didn't understand his jokes! But soon we were good friends. He's very funny and we played a lot of jokes on Angel (Gwen)!'

Bradley James as Arthur

Colin Morgan plays Merlin. Colin is from Ireland and he always wanted to be an actor. 'I was very interested in magic when I was young too,' he says. 'I'm so happy to be Merlin in the show.'

Sometimes Colin had to do difficult things. 'For one of the shows, I had to run into a very cold lake in the rain!' he says. 'Another time I had animal 'dung' – or chocolate! – all over my face!'

Would you like to watch *Merlin*? Why / Why not?

Magical animals

There are a lot of magical animals in *Merlin*. One is the Great Dragon. It lives under Camelot Castle.

Of course, the true star in *Arthur and the Unicorn* is a white horse called Unity – not a unicorn! Unity had to wear a white horn to be the unicorn in the story.

The right castle

Camelot Castle is very important in Merlin. Most of the filming happens there. The film makers looked at castles in England, Scotland, Wales and Eastern Europe but they weren't right. Then they found the Château de Pierrefonds, near Paris in France. Everyone loved it.

What do these words mean? You can use a dictionary.

TV show actor joke / play a joke on lake dung castle horse

THE LEGEND OF

The stories of King Arthur are famous all over the world. But who were Arthur and Merlin? And were the stories true or only legends?

Who was Arthur?

Arthur was a good king many years ago in Britain. King Arthur lived with his beautiful wife, Guinevere, and his brave knights.

Most people think that the stories of King Arthur are only legends. But some say that Arthur lived around the year 500.

Where did Arthur live?

In the legends, Arthur lived in Cornwall, in the south-west of England. The stories say that Arthur was born in Tintagel Castle. You can visit Tintagel Castle today. It's a cold and windy place now, but it is still magical.

King Arthur

What do these words mean? You can use a dictionary.

legend brave knight was born TV show stone round

Tintagel Castle

KING ARTHUR

Who was Merlin?

In the TV show, Merlin is a young man like Arthur. But in the legends, Merlin was an old, clever wizard. He helped Arthur all his life. He took Arthur from his father, Uther Pendragon, when he was a baby. He wanted to protect him.

Merlin and baby Arthur

THE STORIES

There are many stories about Arthur but here are some of the most famous.

The Sword in the Stone

When Arthur was a young boy, he pulled a big sword from a stone. Other knights tried to pull it out, but it was not possible. So everyone knew that Arthur was the new king.

Excalibur

Excalibur

A woman's hand came out of the water with a big sword called Excalibur. She gave the sword to Arthur. Excalibur was magical and it helped Arthur kill many bad people.

The Round Table

King Arthur and his knights sat at the Round Table. Because it was round, no one was first or last. The knights were all the same.

THE PEOPLE

Guinevere was Arthur's beautiful wife, but she also loved Sir Lancelot.

Sir Lancelot was a strong and brave knight. He did many good things.

Sir Mordred was a bad knight. He wanted to be king and killed Arthur in the end.

Sir Galahad was the son of Lancelot. He was Arthur's best knight.

Do you like the stories of King Arthur? What famous legends are there in your country?

MAGICAL

In *Arthur and the Unicorn*, Arthur kills a unicorn. A unicorn isn't a real animal – it's magical. Here are some famous magical animals. Do you know them from stories?

The unicorn

- The unicorn is a beautiful, white animal. It has one long horn on its head.
- The unicorn is a symbol of good. Only bad magic can kill a unicorn.
- Many years ago, people believed that unicorns were real. They often tried to find them.
- The only real animal with one horn is the rhinoceros. Maybe the stories about unicorns started when people first saw the rhinoceros.

The dragon

- The dragon often has the body of a lizard and the feet of an eagle.
- Dragons are sometimes good and sometimes bad!
- In stories, most dragons make fire, can fly and live in caves.

Dragonslayer

ANIMALS

The kraken

Pirates of the Caribbean: Dead Man's Chest

- The kraken is a very big sea animal. It has lots of arms and pulls boats under the water.
- It lives at the bottom of the sea and sleeps. But sometimes it wakes up …
- The kraken is in many films, e.g.*The Clash of the Titans* and the *Pirates of the Caribbean* films.
- There is a real sea animal called the giant squid. Maybe the first story about the kraken was about a giant squid.

Do you know any other magical animals?

The phoenix

- There are stories about the phoenix in many countries, e.g. Greece, Russia, Egypt, China and Japan. All the countries have different stories.
- The Greek phoenix is like an eagle. It is red and gold and sings beautifully.
- In many stories, the phoenix comes to life again. It is a symbol of life after we die.

What do these words mean? You can use a dictionary.

real symbol rhinoceros lizard eagle giant squid gold

CHAPTERS 1–2

Before you read

1 Read 'People and places' on pages 4–5. Answer these questions.
   a) Who is the King of Camelot?
   b) Who is going to be King of Camelot one day?
   c) Who is the King' s doctor?
   d) Who is Arthur's servant?
   e) Who are the two wizards in the story?
   f) Where do Arthur and Uther live?

2 Match the words with the sentences.
   corn   horns   a servant   a storeroom   a unicorn
   a) This animal is magical.
   b) This person cleans and cooks food for someone.
   c) You keep things in this place.
   d) Some animals have these on their heads.
   e) You can make bread with this.

After you read

3 Complete the sentences with these names.
   Anhora   Arthur   Gaius   Merlin   Uther
   a) Merlin lives with … .
   b) … doesn't like magic.
   c) … reads magic books.
   d) The old man in white clothes is … .
   e) … killed the unicorn.

4 Are the sentences true or false? Correct the false sentences.
   a) Uther was angry when Arthur gave him the unicorn's horn.
   b) The corn in the cornfields is green.
   c) There are many bags of corn in the storeroom.
   d) Arthur and Merlin meet Anhora in the storeroom.
   e) Arthur must pass some tests.

5 What do you think?
   a) Does Arthur believe Anhora?
   b) What are the tests going to be?

CHAPTERS 3–4

Before you read

6 Put these words into the sentences.

curse heart kill pride rats

a) … live under people's houses.
b) 'He thinks he is very important – he has too much … .'
c) The old man went to hospital because of a … problem.
d) A sword is used to … .
e) In the story, the corn dies and there is no water. This is because of a … .

After you read

7 Who says these words?

a) 'It was still in the bath!'
b) 'I believe him.'
c) 'I don't want my children to die.'
d) 'Take this, but don't come back!'
e) 'You must have some of this lovely meat!'
f) 'You're not going to be a good king.'
g) 'My people did nothing wrong.'
h) 'Is your pride more important than a man's life?'

8 Answer the questions.

a) Why do Arthur and Merlin go to the storeroom again?
b) Why is Arthur kind to Evan?
c) Why does Merlin think the water comes back?
d) What food does Merlin find for Arthur?
e) Why is Arthur surprised when he sees Evan in the forest?
f) Why does Arthur try to kill Evan?
g) After Evan, who does Arthur see in the forest?

9 What do you think?

a) Who or what is Evan?
b) Arthur tries to kill Evan. Was he right?
c) Do you believe in magic?

CHAPTERS 5–7

Before you read

10 What do you think?

a) Arthur did not pass the tests. What is going to happen now?

b) How can Merlin help Arthur?

After you read

11 Complete each sentence with one of the words

heart horn sword

a) In the Labyrinth Anhora has a … in his hand.

b) Arthur finds love in his … .

c) Arthur and Merlin put the … on the forest floor.

beach forest Labyrinth

d) Merlin follows Arthur to the … .

e) Arthur and Merlin see a unicorn in the … .

f) Arthur's last test is on a … .

give kill protect

g) Arthur wanted to … his life for Merlin.

h) Merlin wanted to … Arthur.

i) It was wrong to … the unicorn.

12 Put the story in the right order.

a) The curse ends.

b) Arthur drinks the poison.

c) The corn in the storeroom is bad.

d) Merlin asks Anhora for one last test.

e) Arthur sees Merlin on a beach.

f) The people wait for food.

g) Merlin meets Anhora in the Labyrinth.

h) Arthur does not die.

13 What do you think?

a) What does Arthur learn in the story?

b) Do you like the story? Why / Why not?